WALKING IN THE SPIRIT
LEADER'S GUIDE

DARING DISCIPLE SERIES

Walking *in* *the* *Spirit*

LEADER'S GUIDE

TERRY POWELL AND BILL JONES

CHRISTIAN PUBLICATIONS, INC.
CAMP HILL, PENNSYLVANIA

CHRISTIAN PUBLICATIONS, INC.
3825 Hartzdale Drive, Camp Hill, PA 17011
www.cpi-horizon.com
www.christianpublications.com

Faithful, biblical publishing since 1883

Walking in the Spirit: Leader's Guide
ISBN: 0-87509-898-3
LOC Control Number: 2001-130445
© Copyright 2001 by
Crossover Communications International.

01 02 03 04 05   5 4 3 2 1

Scripture quotations, unless otherwise indicated, are from the
New American Standard Bible (NASB). © The Lockman
Foundation 1960, 1962, 1963, 1968, 1971,
1972, 1973, 1975, 1977, 1995.

For information, write:
Crossover Communications International
Box 211755
Columbia, SC, USA 29221

NOTE: The Leadership Tips woven throughout this Leader's
Guide are adapted from Terry's book, *You Can Lead a Bible
Discussion Group* (Multnomah Books, 1996).
Used by permission of the author.

CONTENTS

Read This First . . .

It will make a world of difference.

Think for a moment. What is the average church member like? Look at the list below and check which ones you think describe the typical church member.

_____ Unacquainted with his Bible

_____ Unaccustomed to being on his knees

_____ Uninvolved at his church

_____ Unaffected by his preacher

_____ Undecided toward his giving

_____ Unconcerned for his neighbor

_____ Uncommitted to his Lord

_____ Unashamed of his sin

_____ Uninformed about his potential

_____ Unalarmed by his condition

Though it is painful to admit, *most* of these descriptives probably characterize the average church member in America today. This may not give cause for alarm until compared with a list of characteristics that Jesus said should be true of His followers, His disciples:

Desire to become Christlike	Luke 6:40
Insist on loving Christ above all else	Luke 14:26
Sacrifice themselves for cause of Christ	Luke 14:27
Count the cost of commitment	Luke 14:33
Ignore selfish desires	Luke 9:23
Press on in following Christ	Luke 9:23
Learn the truth of God's Word	John 8:31
Express love for other Christians	John 13:34-35
Show forth the fruit of the Spirit	John 15:8

But Why?

Why aren't more Christians today like the early believers found in the New Testament? There are many reasons, but one stands out from the rest. *The Church in America has come close to abandoning Christ's command in Matthew 28:19 to make disciples.* This observation isn't meant to be critical, rather it is meant as a wake-up call—a challenge to make Christ's last command our first priority.

But How?

But how? What does it take to turn an average Christian into a New Testament disciple? According to First Thessalonians 2:1-12, it takes TIME.

T=Teach the Scripture (2:1-6)

Here we find Paul explaining the gospel to the people of Thessalonica. To make a disciple, teaching him the Word of God is absolutely vital. Not only is it "living and active" (Hebrews 4:12), but it's also profitable for teaching, reproof, correction and for training in righteousness. (See 2 Timothy 3:16-17.)

I=Impart Your Life (1 Thessalonians 2:7-8)

Yet Paul felt it wasn't enough simply to teach the Scripture. He poured his life into the people of Thessalonica just as Jesus had poured His life into the disciples. To make a disciple today requires the same process. Teaching the Bible is the beginning, but more is required. You must also pour your life into that other Christian. When it comes to spiritual truth, more is caught from your life than is taught from your lips.

M=Model the Truth (2:9-10)

That is why Paul lived a devout, upright and blameless life. He knew if he taught the Thessalonians to pray, but didn't himself pray, they would never pray either. To make a disciple you too must model the truth. When your time with a discipleship group is over, the members will remember more about how you lived the Christian life than what you said about the Christian life.

E=Encourage Personal Applications (2:11-12)

As Paul taught the Scripture, imparted his life and modeled the truth, he encouraged the Thessalonians to personally apply everything they had learned. He wanted them to walk in a manner worthy of the Lord. The last step to making a disciple is to encourage the person to immediately put into practice what you have taught him. That is what Jesus meant in Matthew 28:20 when He said, "teaching them *to observe* all that I commanded you" (emphasis added).

Over the next three months you will teach the following pages of *Walking in the Spirit*. That's only the first step toward making disciples. Will you take the other three steps? In addition to teaching the Scriptures, will you

- impart your life by spending at least one hour outside the meeting with one or more of the group members for every hour you spend in the meeting?

- model the truth by seeking to live what you teach and be honest when you fall short?

- encourage personal application by encouraging and exhorting your group members?

If you're willing to take these three additional steps, look for the "Leadership Tips" scattered throughout the *Leader's Guide*. These ideas will help you carry out your commitment.

But What?

You may be wondering, "But what difference could these extra steps make?" It could make a significant difference but you must understand up front that it won't happen quickly. That's one reason the Church in America has abandoned Christ's command to make disciples. For most Christians, it takes about two years of TIME for them to become the kind of disciples that the New Testament talks about.

Walking in the Spirit is one in a series of basic discipleship courses offered by Christian Publications.

1st Year Fall—*Knowing God*

Spring—*Discovering Your Identity*

2nd Year Fall—*Walking in the Spirit*

Spring—*Learning to Trust*

If you lead just one person through the first four volumes, it will take you two years. Imagine at the end of those two years if the two of you chose two new people for discipleship: you discipling one and your friend discipling the other. Imagine that you kept discipling just one person every two years and that person in turn did the same. The illustration below shows you what could happen in forty years of disciple making.

Today ....You

2 Years ....You and another

4 Years.............................4 of you

6 Years 8

8 Years 16

10 Years 32

12 Years 64

14 Years 128

16 Years 256

18 Years 512

20 Years 1,024

22 Years	2,048
24 Years	4,096
26 Years	8,192
28 Years	16,384
30 Years	32,786
32 Years	65,536
34 Years	131,072
36 Years	262,144
38 Years	524,288
40 Years	1,048,576 disciples!

And this is only making one disciple every two years! Imagine what could happen multiplying two or three disciple-makers every two years! You would make:

A World of Difference!

Have you caught the vision? With just a little more effort on your part, the meeting moves from a group communicating information to a group facilitating transformation, from a Bible study to a discipleship group.

But Who?

You may be wondering who you should disciple. Begin with those God has led to your group. If you haven't already chosen the members of your group, look for the following persons (list their names on the next page):

_____	_____
_____	_____
_____	_____
_____	_____
_____	_____

When you find these folks, ask them if they will join you and a few other Christians who want to learn the basics of how to grow in their spiritual lives.

But When?

That's the easiest question of all. So easy in fact, you can answer it.

I, (Name) _____,
will begin to make a world of difference by multiplying disciples on (Date) _____.

Getting Acquainted and Course Introduction

Lesson Theme and Objectives

Though the Bible teems with teaching about the Holy Spirit, many Christians approach the subject with fear and trepidation. Worse yet, the controversies and factions that have surfaced over doctrine results in a neglect of the Holy Spirit altogether. *He is too important to dismiss.* And the vast majority of biblical information about the Holy Spirit is *not* controversial. You want participants to see how integral the Holy Spirit is to Christian living and service. Unless they understand and apply the biblical teaching in this course, they'll never rise above the spiritual poverty level.

Strive to accomplish the following objectives in your group's initial meeting:

1. To create a warm, personable atmosphere through the use of a team-building activity.
2. To whet participants' appetites for course content by previewing the questions to be addressed.

3. To identify the distinctive expectations and training philosophy of group meetings.
4. To pray together for life change to occur.

Team Building

Ask participants to share their names, plus the title of a magazine that describes their life over the past few weeks. Tell them to explain the reason for their selection. (If there are more than ten to twelve people in your group, divide into smaller groups for this fellowship activity.) To serve as a catalyst for their thinking, give these examples:

- *Time*—"I haven't had enough of it lately! A recent project my boss gave me has added eight to ten hours to my work week."

- *Changing Times*—"Our last kid left for college last week. We're marveling at how the past few years zoomed by."

- *Decision*—"I figured making decisions would get easier after a while, but I was wrong. Right now I'm wondering if I should change jobs."

Don't hurry this sharing exercise. Encourage participants to ask each other questions. If someone's magazine title reveals a pressing need, stop and pray for him or her. (Point out that building relationships isn't an "appendix" to your group's purpose, but an integral part of it. One distinguishing feature between a church group and a business or civic organization should be the nature of relationships. Experiencing "community" is one factor that sets your group apart as *Christian*.)

Preview of Coming Attractions (10-12 minutes)

In this segment of your meeting, try to seize your group's interest in the subject matter of the *Walking in the Spirit* discipleship book.

First, write the words "Holy Spirit" on a marker board or flip chart. Discuss: **What are some common associations people have when they see or hear the words, "Holy Spirit"?** Encourage negative as well as positive associations. After several people respond, emphasize that the book *Walking in the Spirit*, plus group sessions, will address the various connotations and issues spawned by the words "Holy Spirit." Believers often neglect the doctrine of the Holy Spirit because it is perceived as hard to grasp. Yet by the time group members finish the book and the course, the things they associate with the Holy Spirit will be overwhelmingly positive.

Second, distribute copies of the discipleship book and refer everyone to the table of contents. Instruct them to skim the twelve chapter titles. Discuss: **Which topic are you most interested in examining? Why?**

Course Expectations and Distinctives (8-10 minutes)

Refer participants to Chapter 1 of the *Walking in the Spirit* discipleship book. Each week they will

complete the Bible study exercises in each chapter
before coming to the group session. Each chapter
provides opportunity for their direct discovery in
Scripture, complemented by the authors' input on
the topic. They will also memorize a Bible verse
each week. Point out that their written assignments
and Scripture memorization are *investments*, rather
than *costs*, of course participation.

Next, use the following key words to convey
the training distincitives of this discipleship
course. If possible, use a poster or white board to
display the key words.

1. *Scripture.* The Bible, not human opinion, will
   serve as the group's authority. Discussion questions will stimulate observation, interpretation
   and application of Scripture.
2. *Preparation.* The leader will serve not as a
   lecturer, but as a facilitator. Group members' ad-
   vance preparation will enhance the quality of
   their verbal contributions.
3. *Prayer.* A characteristic of a healthy small group
   is openness. As members share how God's Word
   is affecting them personally, others in the group
   can intercede for them.
4. *Relationships.* The interactive methodology during group sessions, as well as times together outside of the weekly meetings, will foster authentic
   fellowship. Members will learn from each other
   and hold each other accountable for life change.
5. *Application.* The ultimate goal of this group isn't
   simply to learn more truth about the Holy Spirit,

but to learn how to unleash His power in their lives. Both the book and the group sessions will encourage personal carry-over of Bible truths. A combination of challenging questions and anecdotes will help everyone "see" a truth's practical implications.

Conversational Prayers

Chuck Miller once said, "Prayer doesn't just prepare us to minister. Prayer *is* ministry!"[1] Read aloud his maxim regarding prayer. Point out that group prayer times will be an integral part of the course. The ultimate purpose of the book and group sessions is *life change*, and prayer taps into the power of the Spirit so life changes can occur. Invite several volunteers to pray aloud and intercede for life changes to happen as a result of truths they discover about the Holy Spirit. Also ask participants to pray for you as you prepare for and lead the group meetings.

Looking Ahead

Assign Chapter 1 in the discipleship book, which introduces them to the Person of the Holy Spirit. Remind them to bring their completed assignments each week, as well as their Bible and a pen. You may want to distribute a sheet of paper and get everyone's name, address and phone number to facilitate communication and relationship building.

LEADERSHIP TIP

You want God's Word to sift through you as a leader before you and your group sift through God's Word together. That's the sequence Paul had in mind for Timothy: "Pay close attention to yourself and to your teaching" (1 Timothy 4:16). As you prepare for group meetings, approach the Bible passage(s) in each lesson devotionally, *before* you glance at the lesson plan we provide. To accelerate your personal application of the Bible texts you teach, jot down responses to the following questions.

- *How does this passage increase my appreciation for God the Father, Jesus Christ or the Holy Spirit?*

- *What reasons for praising the Lord does the text offer?*

- *What sin to avoid or to forsake does the content expose?*

- *What positive course of action does the passage propose?*

- *What bearing do these verses have on my prayer life?*

- *What encourages me from the passage? Why?*

- *What circumstances, decisions or people come to mind as I read? Why?*

If one or more of these questions pry open your heart and reveal practical implications for your life, they can have the same effect on your group members. If you find reasons for praise or encouragement in the text, so can they. If you spot a connection between a verse and your prayer life, so can they. So when you come across a productive devotional question as part of your personal preparation, insert it into that week's lesson plan.

Who Is the Holy Spirit?

Lesson Theme and Objectives

Due to controversies surrounding the subject of the Holy Spirit, Christians often study Him superficially or avoid the doctrine altogether. But we can't be good stewards of Scripture and treat the Holy Spirit casually. He is too prominent in God's Word to take a shallow approach to studying His role in Scripture and the lives of Christians.

The first question we must answer concerns the identity of the Holy Spirit. Chapter 1 of *Walking in the Spirit* discusses who He is and provides evidence of His personhood and His deity.

When your group meets, strive to accomplish these objectives:

1. To discover what the analogy of "jumping" a dead battery says about the Holy Spirit.
2. To identify characteristics of the Holy Spirit that are similar to human traits.
3. To identify divine characteristics of the Holy Spirit that distinguish Him from human beings.
4. To define and illustrate the concept of the Trinity.
5. To discuss practical implications of His personhood for daily Christian living.

Group Accountability (2-4 Minutes)

This section of each lesson will suggest a way to establish accountability for the application ideas of previous lessons. Personal testimonies, Scripture memory recitation and reviews of follow-through ideas are among the recommended strategies offered. This week, pair off and ask everyone to recite John 14:16-17 to his partner.

Approach the Word (6-8 Minutes)

Display a jumper cable. Ask: **How is the basic function of the Holy Spirit similar to that of a jumper cable?**

As the introduction to Chapter 1 in the discipleship book points out, the word Jesus employed for the Holy Spirit meant "one who comes alongside to help." Just as rejuvenating power flows through the cable from a strong battery to a weaker one, the Holy Spirit "comes alongside" and infuses us with God's power when we need it most. He enables us to function on all cylinders, spiritually speaking. Chapter 1 addresses the most fundamental question of all: **Who is the Holy Spirit?**

Absorb the Word (30-40 Minutes)

Comparison to Humanity

To cover the content in the "Comparison to Humanity" sections in *Walking in the Spirit*, employ the following questions. Refer to the authors' commentary and your own answers to the study exercises to supplement their responses as needed.

Discuss: **What misconceptions about the Holy Spirit are prevalent?**

The primary point of Chapter 1 can be summarized in a sentence. Ask a volunteer to fill in the blanks verbally:

The Holy Spirit is a _____, not a _____.

- **What are the three basic aspects of human personality?**

- **How does the Holy Spirit exhibit these characteristics?**

- **In what ways can our treatment of the Holy Spirit compare to our treatment of other people?**

Characteristics of Divinity

The "Characteristics of Divinity" section makes a case for the deity of the Holy Spirit. Rather than rehash each of the questions in the discipleship book, solicit personal impressions from group members with the following:

- **Which divine attribute of the Holy Spirit impresses you most? Why?**

- **Which divine characteristic of the Holy Spirit do you find most encouraging? Why? Most convicting? Why?**

Functions of Divinity

The Holy Spirit's divine status is seen in His works as well as in His qualities. Ask:

- How is the Holy Spirit's creative capacity different from the creative ability of humans?

- How did His inspiration of Scripture differ from the inspiration that motivates contemporary human authors?

- How was the Spirit's involvement in Jesus' conception different from natural human births?

- What aspect of an evangelistic or Bible teaching ministry is reserved for the Holy Spirit?

Three in One

To unravel the mystery of the Trinity is a difficult task. Yet no resource on the Holy Spirit is complete without referring to His place in the Godhead. Give participants a moment to skim this part of their books again. Then ask:

- Which statement or concept did you find most helpful? Why?

- Which analogy sheds the most light on this biblical concept?

To the material in the discipleship book add the following information regarding the relationship among members of the Trinity.

The heart of Christian faith in God is the revealed mystery of the Trinity. *Trinitas* is a Latin word meaning *three-ness*. Christianity rests on the three-ness, the tri-personality of God. . . .

The Son is subject to the Father, for the Son is sent by the Father in His (the Father's) name (John 3:16; 5:23).

The Spirit is subject to the Father, for the Spirit is sent by the Father in the Son's name (14:16, 26).

The Spirit is subject to the Son as well as to the Father, for the Spirit is sent by the Son as well as by the Father (15:26).

The Spirit came to exercise the ministry of a Comforter in Christ's stead (14:16). If the ministry of Christ the Comforter was important, the ministry of the Holy Spirit the Comforter can scarcely be less important. . . . It is an extraordinary thing that those who profess to care so much about Christ should know and care so little about the Holy Spirit.[1]

Apply the Word (6-8 Minutes)

The remark by Paul Little at the start of Chapter 1 in the discipleship book summarizes the main point: *the Holy Spirit is a Person, not a substance.*

To wrap up this session, brainstorm as a group for practical implications of the Holy Spirit's personhood. Ask: **What difference should viewing the Holy Spirit as a Person make in our lives?** To their contributions, add the following suggestions as needed:

- We should be motivated to learn what God's Word teaches about Him.

- We should be more sensitive to the effect our decisions and conduct have on Him.

- We should maintain awareness of our daily need for His power.

- We should feel appreciation and confidence as a result of His presence within us.

To close, pray that group members will experience these practical implications as they proceed through this course.

Looking Ahead

Assign Chapter 2, which examines in more detail what the Holy Spirit does.

 LEADERSHIP TIP

One way to mobilize workers for God's kingdom is to cultivate an *equipping mind-set*—to serve as a trainer who passes along the concepts and skills you've acquired. That's what Paul had in mind when he wrote, "The things which you have heard from me . . . entrust these to faithful men who will be able to teach others also" (2 Timothy 2:2, emphasis added).

Here's where we're going with all this: *Don't just lead successful discipleship groups. Keep an eye out for folks you can train for a similar ministry.* Candidates for your training investment include members of your current group. Perhaps you can groom a participant to lead his or her own group upon completion of this course. Preparing someone else to lead a separate group is the closest you'll ever come to being in two places at once.

What Does the Holy Spirit Do? (Part 1)

Lesson Theme and Objectives

This is the first of two group sessions focusing on the work of the Holy Spirit. This lesson emphasizes what the Holy Spirit has accomplished for believers in the process of conversion. Ask the Lord to facilitate accomplishment of these objectives:

1. To identify past works of the Holy Spirit on behalf of believers.
2. To feel encouraged by a greater awareness of our privileged status in relation to God.
3. To express gratitude to God for the ministries of the Holy Spirit that brought us into the family of God.

Group Accountability (3-5 Minutes)

First, ask a review question stemming from your last session: **What practical implications of the Holy Spirit's personhood did we cite?** (To supplement their responses, see the "Apply the Word" segment in Lesson 1 of this Leader's Guide.)

Second, divide into pairs and ask everyone to recite John 7:37-39.

Approach the Word (5-7 Minutes)

Read aloud the following quotation:

> Religious instruction, however sound, is not enough by itself. It brings light, but it cannot impart sight. . . . The assumption that light and sight are synonymous has brought spiritual tragedy to millions. . . . The Pharisees looked straight at the Light of the World for three years, but not one ray of light reached their inner beings. Light is not enough. . . . The inward operation of the Holy Spirit is necessary to saving faith. The gospel is light but only the Spirit can give sight.[1]

Discuss: **What is the connection between this quotation and today's Bible study?**

The quote mentions the "inward operation of the Holy Spirit" in the process of Christian conversion. Today's study shines the spotlight on this process and identifies specific ways in which the Spirit works within us to bring us to God.

Absorb the Word (30-35 Minutes)

To Cover "Past Performances"

The Bible study exercises in Chapter 2 exposed group members to five past works of the Holy Spirit. Begin this phase of your meeting by referring to the five sets of Bible verses in the "Past Performances" section of the book, Chapter 2. **Ask volun-**

teers to tell what words/phrases they found that describe the Spirit's activity. Be aware that precise terminology may differ, depending on which Bible translations members use. The remainder of the book chapter and this group session will define the biblical concepts and their practical implications.

To Cover "He Regenerates Your Spirit"

Invite volunteers to share their responses to the questions in this section (page 18 of the discipleship book). Emphasize that divine initiative in regeneration elevates the grace of God and our own unworthiness. Ask a group member to read aloud Ephesians 2:1-9, which describes God's initiative and contrasts our spiritual state before and after salvation. Our logical response is one of gratitude or praise. "For You, O LORD, have made me glad by what You have done" (Psalm 92:4).

To Cover "He Indwells Your Body"

Refer group members again to First Corinthians 6:16-20. Let several read their answers to this question: **The Holy Spirit resides within us. What is the significance of that truth for *your* daily life?**

In First Corinthians 6, Paul gave a rationale for sexual purity among Christians. A person who lives with a keen awareness of the Holy Spirit's presence is less likely to defile his body, which is the Spirit's temple or sanctuary. The Spirit's residency also denotes divine ownership of our lives. Since we belong to God, our own "rights" over our physical bodies have been relinquished. What we do with our bodies either glorifies or grieves the Lord.

This part of Chapter 2 ended with a question for personal evaluation. Pause for a few minutes, allowing participants time to pray silently in view of their analysis of the past twenty-four hours.

To Cover "He Seals Your Future"

Give participants a moment to review the content of this section of their book. Then ask them to read Philippians 1:6: "For I am confident of this very thing, that He who began a good work in you will perfect it until the day of Christ Jesus." Ask: **How does Philippians 1:6 summarize the Spirit's work of sealing our future?**

Also, instruct group members to skim this section of Chapter 2 to formulate answers to these questions:

- **How are feelings about our relationship with God sometimes in conflict with objective reality?**

- **How can the concept of the Spirit's *sealing* help someone who feels spiritually insecure?**

To Review "He Guarantees Your Inheritance"

In Ephesians 1:14 and Second Corinthians 1:22, Paul called the Holy Spirit a "pledge." Ask:

- **How was the term "pledge" employed in the business arena of Paul's day?**

- How is the business background of the term analogous to the work of the Holy Spirit?

Supplement their responses as you deem necessary from the analogies supplied in this section of the book. Then solicit volunteer responses to the question they tackled in the book: **Which aspect of the analogy means most to you? Why?**

To Review "He Records Your Membership"

Read First Corinthians 12:13 aloud:

- **What are some common misconceptions of the phrase "baptism of the Holy Spirit"?**

- **In this verse, what does the metaphor of baptism represent?**

How the Holy Spirit Helped Jesus

To beef up your emphasis on the past work of the Spirit on behalf of believers, talk briefly about how the Holy Spirit worked in the life of Jesus Christ. (This material is not in the discipleship book.) Study the Bible references that follow, and elaborate a bit on each work of the Holy Spirit that is mentioned.

1. Luke 1:35—The Holy Spirit brought about Jesus' miraculous birth.
2. Luke 3:22—The Holy Spirit visibly identified with Jesus.
3. Luke 4:1—The Holy Spirit guided Jesus.
4. Luke 4:18-19; 5:17—The Holy Spirit enabled Jesus to preach and to heal the sick.

5. Romans 8:11—The Holy Spirit raised Jesus from the dead.
6. Hebrews 9:14—The Holy Spirit accomplished Jesus' sacrificial death.[2]

Apply the Word (10-12 Minutes)

Divide into smaller groups of three or four persons. Ask participants to share their written responses to the questions in the "Personal Reflections" section of Chapter 2 (pages 25-26). Before dispersing, encourage members of each group to pray conversationally, expressing gratitude for what the Holy Spirit has done for them.

Looking Ahead

Read aloud the illustration featuring Dwight L. Moody from Chapter 3 of *Walking in the Spirit* (page 27). Point out that Moody's life shows that the Spirit's activity is *not* limited to the process of conversion. Tell them to finish Chapter 3, which identifies things the Holy Spirit can do for them in the here and now.

LEADERSHIP TIP

Discipleship groups provide fertile soil for the development of new teachers and facilitators. To spot budding leaders within your current group, mull over the following questions and see who comes to mind.

- *Who demonstrates commitment to the group through regular attendance and consistent completion of assignments?*

- *Who participates regularly without monopolizing the conversation?*

- *Who shows sensitivity to other participants by complimenting their insight or probing for their views on a subject?*

- *Whose answers to study questions reveal keen analysis and concern for sound Bible interpretation?*

- *Who exhibits an infectious enthusiasm for God's Word?*

- *In response to questions, who articulates in a clear, compelling manner?*

- *Whose answers do the other group members respect the most?*

What Does the Holy Spirit Do? (Part 2)

Lesson Theme and Objectives

In your last meeting you examined *past* activity of the Holy Spirit in relation to believers' coming to Christ. The five truths you studied solidified participants' position in relationship to God. Now the focus shifts to *present* ministries of the Holy Spirit. These "exceptional" works are benefits they can appropriate daily in their spiritual pilgrimages. Through the learning activities that follow, seek to accomplish these objectives:

1. To identify ways in which the Holy Spirit currently works on our behalf.
2. To determine ways to cooperate with God and expedite experience of these works of the Holy Spirit.

Group Accountability (6-8 Minutes)

Ask group members to describe the physical setting in which they completed the assignments in Chapter 3. (Were they at a desk in a home office? At a kitchen table? In a recliner with the network news on TV in the background?) Emphasize the importance of preparing each week's assignment in a location free from distractions and interruptions. *Also encourage them to complete each chapter in one sitting, if possible.* Reserving one forty-five- to sixty-minute time slot will result in a more focused and less disjointed effort than completing the assignment over several days in ten to twelve minute segments.

Next, ask everyone to meet with a partner and recite the memory verses: Luke 4:1, 14.

Approach the Word (2-3 Minutes)

The following remarks by J. Sidlow Baxter refer to the work of the Holy Spirit. Read the quote aloud.

> Who God chooses, He cleanses.
> Who God cleanses, He molds.
> Who God molds, He fills.
> Who God fills, He uses.[1]

To provide transition into the Bible study, point out that being filled and used by the Holy Spirit requires awareness of His potential ministries in our lives. What follows are six ways in which He yearns to work in every Christian's life.

Absorb the Word (30-40 Minutes)

To Cover "Present Potential"

In this section of the discipleship book, participants examined five sets of Bible verses and recorded words/phrases highlighting current ministries of the Holy Spirit. Ask a different volunteer to tell what words/phrases he or she found in each set of references. (Precise terminology may differ, depending on which Bible translations members use.) This phase of your Bible study is *observation* of the selected verses. The remainder of the session will involve the group in *interpreting* and *applying* the observations.

To Cover "He Assures Your Heart"

Encourage group members to glean answers to the following questions from the commentary in this part of the discipleship book.

In what kinds of situations is this first work of the Spirit most helpful for a believer?

This ministry of assurance is an inward subjective experience. **How can we know that it's valid or reliable?**

Failing the Lord may instill doubts about the reality of our salvation. **What provision has the Lord made to help Christians who fail?**

To Cover "He Helps You Understand the Bible"

Ask for a volunteer to define the Bible truth of *illumination.* Then ask: **What difference between a Christian and a non-Christian did Paul cite in First Corinthians 2:11-12?**

What is one application of realizing our need for the Spirit's illumination of Scripture? (Emphasize the need to pray and ask God to clarify our thinking as we read His Word.)

Here's how one author amplified the Spirit's
work of illumination. Read this excerpt aloud at
this point in the lesson:

> Because the Holy Spirit comprehends the depth of
> God's nature, He is competent to reveal the things
> of God to man. . . . The word for "know" in 1 Co-
> rinthians 2:12 suggests that, because of the teaching
> work of the Holy Spirit, believers possess an inher-
> ent knowledge of the things of God revealed in His
> Word—things that eye, ear, and heart are unable to
> know or comprehend through seeing, hearing or
> feeling.[2]

To Clarify "He Comforts Your Emotions"

How do the verses from John's Gospel (see discipleship book) indicate the Holy Spirit's ministry
of comfort?

Who can share a time when you experienced the
comforting work of God's Spirit? (Be sure respon-
dents describe the means He used to provide comfort.
Did He employ a Bible verse? Did He encourage during a time of prayer? Through another Christian?)

Also ask for brief testimonials in response to
the last question in this section of the discipleship
book: How can the Holy Spirit's ministry of comfort strengthen your witness to unbelievers whom
you know? (Use Paul and Silas' experience in jail
to illustrate the outreach potential of the Spirit's
comfort during adversity: Acts 16:22-30.)

"He Intercedes for You"

First, seek responses to the question at the beginning of this section in the discipleship book. Em-

phasize that when we yearn to talk to God but can't find the right words, remembering Romans 8:26-27 encourages us. We realize that due to the Spirit's intercession, God understands our hearts and hears our need.

Instruct them to think about the future and painful situations that people sometimes encounter.

In what types of circumstances will we need to recall the truth of Romans 8:26-27?

To Explain "He Guides You"

Discuss: **What are some occasions when we need the Holy Spirit's guidance? Who can share a time when you clearly received the guiding ministry of the Holy Spirit?**

To Teach "He Empowers Your Life And Ministry"

Discuss: **Where does the Holy Spirit fit into a quest for personal holiness and effective ministry?**

This part of the discipleship book points out that you are neither left alone in your quest for character nor in your efforts to serve the Lord. Read aloud Philippians 2:13, which suggests that God enables us for whatever He calls us to do. Ask: **How does awareness of this fact make you feel? Why?**

After asking for volunteers to answer the question on Colossians 1:28-29, give the following definition: *The Christian life is my giving out whatever God is putting in.* **What thoughts or feelings about the Christian life or ministry do you have after reading the story of A.J. Gordon?**

Apply the Word (8-10 Minutes)

To wrap up this meeting, divide into groups of three or four people. Instruct the groups to share answers to the three questions in the "Personal Reflections" section of the discipleship book. Then they can pray for one another in view of the needs disclosed during discussion of the second question.

Before dispersing, encourage members to pray on their own, *telling the Holy Spirit*, rather than telling God the Father or the Lord Jesus Christ, how thankful they are for the works cited in this lesson.[3]

Looking Ahead

Assign Chapter 4. Point out that they will discover the reason for "power shortages" in the lives and ministries of many believers. Also, ask the group members to keep a journal during the week, recording instances when they experience the Holy Spirit's work in their lives.

LEADERSHIP TIP

Over the years, you have probably acquired ministry competence in areas such as personal evangelism, Bible teaching, small group leadership and planning. The last two "Leadership Tips" in this *Leader's Guide* have encouraged you to perceive yourself as a trainer—one who reproduces in others the competencies you yourself have acquired. The previous tip offered criteria for spotting potential small group leaders. Now it is time to give you a fixed series of operations that a trainer utilizes in transferring a ministry skill or leadership proficiency.

- *I CAN DO IT. The leader has experience and some degree of expertise in the skill to be imparted.*

- *I DO IT WHILE OTHERS WATCH. The leader demonstrates the ability. By observing, others pick up nuances and procedures that accelerate their acquisition of the skill.*

- *WE DO IT TOGETHER. The leader delegates a limited amount of responsibility to others. The leader and trainees plan and implement an event or method as a team. The apprentices gradually gain self-confidence. The difficulty and amount of their responsibility increase in small increments.*

- *THEY DO IT WHILE I WATCH. The leader becomes the observer while learners go solo. The leader stays around to offer encouragement and evaluative feedback.*

- *THEY DO IT. (And the cycle keeps repeating itself.)*

How does this training cycle apply to your development of new disciple-makers? To your mentoring of people who want to learn how to witness?

Why Am I Not Experiencing the Holy Spirit's Power?

Lesson Theme and Objectives

A Christian leader named A.C. Dixon re-marked,

> When we rely on organization, we get what organization can do. When we rely on education, we get what education can do. When we rely on eloquence, we get what eloquence can do. But when we rely on the Holy Spirit, we get what *God* can do.[1]

Bull's-eye! Whether the need is growth in holiness or fruitfulness in ministry, the Holy Spirit is the One who empowers us to excel. The typical church member is not tapping into the Holy Spirit's power. Spiritual poverty, not spiritual plenty, is the more familiar condition. Strive to achieve these specific lesson objectives:

1. To identify the extent of spiritual poverty in the church.
2. To discuss reasons for spiritual poverty.
3. To determine characteristics of a person not experiencing the Holy Spirit's power.
4. To uncover Paul's advice for overcoming spiritual poverty.

Group Accountability (8-10 Minutes)

In your previous meeting you identified what the Holy Spirit does in and for the believer. To conclude the last session you asked group members to keep a journal during the week, recording instances when they experienced His work on their behalf. Perhaps God's Spirit comforted or convicted them during a devotional study of Scripture. Perhaps He supplied wisdom needed for a decision or moved in the heart of an unbeliever with whom they shared the gospel. At this time, ask for brief testimonials of the Holy Spirit's activity in their lives since you last met. To keep the reports biblical rather than excessively subjective, ask for illustrations of His works cited in last week's lesson.

Then pair off and ask each person to recite the memory verse: Galatians 5:19-21.

Approach the Word (3-5 Minutes)

To launch this week's topic, communicate the story that follows to your group.

As he prepared for a sermon, a pastor was studying John chapter 14. In that chapter he observed three references to knowing the members of the Trinity. In verse 7 he saw that Jesus referred to knowing God the Father and he also noted a phrase which spoke of the disciples' knowledge of Jesus—God the Son. The third reference was in verse 17, which spoke of the disciples' knowing the Holy Spirit—God the Spirit.

As he observed these references to knowing the members of the Trinity, the pastor mused:

> I know God the Father . . . and have experienced much of His paternal love and care. I know God the Son, for is He not my Savior with whom I daily commune? But I cannot say that I know the Holy Spirit in any comparable and personal way.[2]

This reflection on John 14 led the pastor to a more comprehensive study of the Holy Spirit in Scripture. The result was an *experiential* knowledge of Him that had been lacking in his life.

After sharing this story, emphasize that even Christian leaders often take the Holy Spirit and His ministry for granted. Yet a right relationship with Him is the secret to power in holiness as well as service. This session illuminates the causes, characteristics and cure for the spiritual poverty that stems from neglecting the Holy Spirit.

Absorb the Word (30-35 Minutes)

Read Andrew Murray's observation of most Christians found in the discipleship book. Discuss:

- **Which evidence of spiritual poverty left the biggest impression on you? Why?**

- **What additional symptoms of spiritual impoverishment do you see among professing Christians?**

Before going to the section on "Causes of Spiritual Poverty," ask rhetorically: **Have you ever thought victorious Christian living was a special de-**

luxe edition of Christianity to be enjoyed only by a select few?

Causes of Spiritual Poverty

Briefly review the three causes of spiritual poverty presented in this chapter: 1) lack of the Holy Spirit's presence in their lives; 2) lack of instruction about the Holy Spirit's potential; and 3) lack of obedience to God's will in Scripture.

Regarding cause #1, ask:

- **What is the basic difference between these two responses to the gospel: a) mentally acknowledging the truth about Jesus Christ; and b) saving faith in Christ?**
- **How do the Bible verses on demons help illustrate the difference?**

Emphasize that the Holy Spirit indwells every person from the moment of conversion and that a non-Christian doesn't have access to the Holy Spirit or His power.

Regarding cause #2, ask: **What accounts for a convert's ignorance about the Holy Spirit's presence or potential?** (A lack of biblical teaching on the Holy Spirit.) Point out that an awareness of the Spirit's presence at conversion does not automatically result in an experience of His power.

Participants delved into Romans 8:10-13 for answers to two questions. Solicit volunteer responses at this time. The following phrases from the passage reveal the Holy Spirit's potential effects: "will also give life to your mortal bodies through His Spirit"

(8:11); and "if by the Spirit you are putting to death the deeds of the body, you will live" (8:13).

Regarding cause #3: The authors state that even a mature Christian can get complacent and experience a "riches to rags" story. We can choose to disregard spiritual practices, which leaves us vulnerable to temptations that we have overcome for years. **Let several group members share their reaction to this possibility, as recorded in their discipleship book. Then ask them to identify positive outcomes that such an awareness may have.** (Knowing that a moral collapse is a possibility should engender a healthy distrust of our sinful nature. The result should be a sober attitude, an ever-increasing reliance on Bible study, prayer and fellowship.)

Characteristics of Spiritual Poverty

To discuss this section of the discipleship book, divide into groups of three. Ask learners to share with one another their responses to the three questions on Romans 7:14-24. The last question in this section requires a lot of honesty and transparency. Give them formal permission to pass on it or to put their responses in the form of a prayer request. Then someone else in the group can pray for the need disclosed.

Apply the Word (12-15 Minutes)

Conquering Spiritual Poverty

Tell participants to consult their discipleship books to answer this question: **What two types of Christians does Paul describe in Galatians 5:16-18?**

Refer the group back to the story about a man carrying a heavy burden who, after catching a ride on a wagon, refused to put down his burden. Ask: **How does this simple story help you understand the difference between Christians who walk according to the flesh and those who walk according to the Spirit?**

Also discuss:

- **Why would some Christians *not* want to escape spiritual poverty?**

- **What would be your greatest motivation for escaping spiritual poverty and appropriating the Holy Spirit's power for your life and ministry?**

Looking Ahead

Emphasize that the next few lessons cover the concept of walking in the Spirit in more specific terms. They will discover *how* to experience more of the Holy Spirit's power for daily living and effective ministry. Also assign the next memory verse: *Ephesians 4:30.*

LEADERSHIP TIP
"TOP Notch Teaching"

How does a person learn to teach or lead a small group Bible study? Acquiring any ministry skill involves three primary processes:

- *T=Training*
- *O=Observing*
- *P=Practicing*

Training is the instruction and assistance you receive from a mentor or experienced leader. It's the acquisition of knowledge plus know-how that serves as a prerequisite for honing a skill. Training takes a variety of forms: attending a leadership development course or seminar, reading a book, watching a how-to video or participating in one-on-one discipleship, to name a few.

Observing is the intentional effort to learn from a model. You watch as an experienced leader demonstrates the skills you hope to acquire. Observation is a specific aspect of the broader concept of training. You are more apt to perfect a skill if you repeatedly see it exhibited.

Practicing is a rehearsal of the skill you hope to develop. To increase the likelihood of success, practice should occur in a supportive setting, with evaluative feedback from a supervisor.

The first letters of the three key words spell TOP. Applying these three processes to your development of workers should result in "TOP notch" lay leadership. Mull over this question: How can I incorporate all three processes in my training of new discipleship group leaders?

How Do I Grieve the Holy Spirit?

Lesson Theme and Objectives

W hat makes one's experience of grief possible is love. We only grieve when someone we love experiences pain or behaves in a way that causes us pain. God's unconditional love for us is the basis for the Holy Spirit's grieving over our sins. The first step in overcoming any sin is to view that sin from God's perspective and to regret causing Him pain. Allow the following objectives to serve as a guiding mechanism for your group meeting:

1. To identify ways in which we can grieve the Holy Spirit.
2. To discuss consequences of surrendering to deeds of the flesh.
3. To discuss strategies for overcoming specific deeds of the flesh.

Group Accountability (3-5 Minutes)

Ask a volunteer to recite the memory verse: *Ephesians 4:30.* If other participants memorized it from different translations, ask one or two others to recite their version as well. Then discuss the verse:

- Ephesians 4:30 is in the form of a *command*. What are the implications of Paul's use of an imperative?

- According to Ephesians 4:30, why does Paul tell us not to grieve the Holy Spirit?

Approach the Word (5-7 Minutes)

Remind group members that *grieve* is a love word meaning to cause pain for someone who cares deeply for us. Then divide into pairs. Ask everyone to share with his partner a time when he either experienced grief or caused someone else grief. After several minutes, point out that we can grieve the Holy Spirit. Grieving Him is possible because God loves us so much. This lesson focuses on ways we grieve God and how to avoid causing Him pain.

Absorb the Word (35-40 Minutes)

The Bible study activities in the discipleship book zero in on Galatians 5:19-21. Grieving the Holy Spirit occurs when we engage in "deeds of the flesh." This Scripture selection lists representative deeds that characterize either an unsaved person or a believer who is out of fellowship with the Lord. Before delving into that list, ask: **Why is it impossible to walk in the Spirit and walk in the flesh simultaneously?** (Galatians 5:17 suggests the answer. Since fleshly and Spirit-led desires are polar opposites, they cannot prompt the same behavior.)

Devote the majority of your discussion time to the "Ways We Grieve God" section of the discipleship book. What follows is a recommended procedure.

First, bring to the group meeting several recent issues of a city newspaper (or *USA Today*). You'll need one copy or issue for every two or three people. Ask group members to skim the headlines and find examples of the "deeds of the flesh" mentioned in Galatians 5:19-21. After three to five minutes, ask for volunteers to cite articles/events that illustrate lifestyle characteristics referred to in Galatians 5:19-21.

Use this activity to emphasize the timeless nature of today's topic. What characterized an individual or a culture apart from Christ in the first century still describes human nature today. To reinforce what mankind is like apart from the influence of God's Spirit, read aloud the following Bible verses: Jeremiah 17:5, 9; and Mark 7:20-23. Also point out that "deeds of the flesh" may not be a *pattern* for most Christians.

This Bible study will help participants evaluate their attitudes and actions so a greater degree of purity can be achieved. Warn them that it is possible for Christians to experience a moral erosion that will ruin their testimony and cause the Lord grief. Perhaps the Bible study will serve as a preventive measure for them.

To Cover "Ways We Grieve God"

Give group members a few minutes to skim the "Ways We Grieve God" section of their books. They answered questions on specific deeds of the flesh and received commentary that deepened their understanding of terms. To rehash every question contained in the discipleship book is unnecessary. Instead, ask selected questions to spur meaningful discussion of the Bible content.

- **In what ways can you categorize these various deeds of the flesh?** (Possible categories include *sexual* sins, *verbal* sins, sins of *thought* as well as *deed*, sins damaging *interpersonal relationships*, plus *behaviors linked to alcohol abuse*.)

- **Which "deed of the flesh" from the list do you believe is most prevalent among professing Christians? Why?**

- *Immorality, impurity* and *sensuality* are the products of a contaminated heart. Discuss this question from the discipleship book: **What are some concrete ways to guard or watch over our hearts?**

- Regarding *idolatry*: **Why is greed (or covetousness) synonymous with idolatry?**

- Eight different terms, each with a different shade of meaning, show what happens to relationships when people aren't Spirit-filled: *enmities, strife, jealousy, outbursts of anger, disputes, dissension, factions* and *envyings*. Several questions couched in this section of the book deal with preventing or minimizing relational problems. Ask volunteers to share responses to these probes: **What attitudes or behaviors can prevent strife? Why are we to avoid hot-tempered people? According to Proverbs 15:1, what approach can relieve or minimize a dispute?**

To Cover "Deterrents to Grieving the Spirit"

- **According to Romans 6:6-7, why is "yielding to the flesh" not inevitable?**
- **What past act has freed us from slavery to sin as a pattern of life?**
- **Why is obeying First John 1:9 a deterrent to grieving the Holy Spirit?**

To supplement their answers, emphasize that Christ's crucifixion and resurrection have practical implications for our capacity to resist sin. In a mysterious yet very real way, we died with Him on the cross and we were raised to a new life when He was resurrected! When we do fail Him, immediate confession restores our fellowship with God. Any act of sin hurts Him but He is grieved even more when we refuse to acknowledge sin.

Before moving to the application based on this week's memory verse, give participants a couple of minutes to pray silently, confessing any sin that may be grieving the Holy Spirit right now.

Apply the Word (5-7 Minutes)

In the "Memorizing Scripture and Application" section of the discipleship book, participants discovered a grammatical link between Ephesians 4:30

and the preceding verse. *The clear implication is that one way we grieve the Holy Spirit is misuse of our tongue.* Our daily conversations either please the Lord or hurt Him. Close by sharing the following guidelines for speech. Each guideline is rooted in a separate phrase from Ephesians 4:29. Encourage your group to jot down these guidelines and keep them in their Bible—or better yet on a card near their telephone.

God's Philosophy of Conversation

- **Are any of my words impure or unwholesome?**
- **Do my words build up or tear down other people?**
- **Do my words meet needs?**
- **Do my words give grace to those who hear or about whom I'm talking?**

Close in prayer. Ask the Lord to keep everyone's heart tender and sensitive to the effect that sins have upon the heart of God.

Looking Ahead

Whet their appetite for the next chapter by reading aloud this quote from the first page of Chapter 6 in the discipleship book: "The greatest unused power in the world is the Holy Spirit of the living God." Point out that Chapter 6 tells why the Holy Spirit's power is often untapped.

LEADERSHIP TIP
Team Building

One feature that distinguishes a church group from a civic organization should be the nature of relationships. That is why "team building" is an integral part of the agenda for church training events. Team building is any structured or intentional effort to improve the experience of fellowship among participants. The time you reserve for team building isn't an appendix to your meeting or an optional "warm fuzzy." Rather it is what sets your group apart as *Christian*.

Start a file of mixers, get-acquainted games and creative activities that promote sharing and increase familiarity among trainees. Two sources of ideas are books you read and workshops you attend. Whether you come across an idea while reading or you're present when someone else implements it, jot down the procedure and keep it for future use.

The introductory lesson in this *Leader's Guide* suggests a get-acquainted activity (a magazine title that describes your life over the past few weeks). Here's another idea not mentioned before in this guide.

Designer Name Tag. Ask everyone to write or print his name in the shape of something that describes what he is like, or some interest or hobby he has. Give examples before asking members to proceed. (A fellow who enjoys basketball could print his name in the shape of a circle. A person wrestling with a major decision could form a question mark with the letters of his name.) Giving each person a few minutes to display and explain his design is an effective way to exchange personal information.

How Do I Quench
the Holy Spirit?

Lesson Theme and Objectives

We quench the Holy Spirit when we nullify or restrict His power in our lives. By resisting what He wants to do for us, in us and through us, we extinguish the flame of His activity. This lesson defines the concept of "quenching" the Spirit, shows *how* we inhibit His work in our lives, then examines deterrents to quenching the Spirit. Pray for the fulfillment of the following objectives:

1. To determine the difference between *grieving* the Spirit and *quenching* the Spirit.
2. To discuss ways we refuse what the Spirit wants to do *for us*, reject what He wants to do *in us* and resist what He yearns to do *through us*.
3. To evaluate our use of Scripture as a fuel supply for God's Spirit.
4. To increase our sensitivity to the Holy Spirit through a growing awareness of His inner promptings.
5. To identify the Bible's role in helping us discern the reliability of inner promptings or subjective impressions.

Group Accountability (3-5 Minutes)

The previous lesson examined deeds of the flesh which grieve the Holy Spirit. Ask the group to reflect on their activities, relationships, conversations and thought life since the last group session. Read First John 1:9 aloud and remind them of the importance of confessing our sins as a way of keeping our hearts soft. Devote several minutes to silent praying, giving those who need it an opportunity to ask for forgiveness.

Next, tell everyone to find a partner and recite this week's memory verse: *First Thessalonians 5:19.*

Approach the Word (3-5 Minutes)

Bring a large candle and a match to your group session. Light the candle, then extinguish the flame by smothering it with a wet rag. Ask: **How does that demonstration clarify the concept of "Do not quench the Spirit" from First Thessalonians 5:19?** After you receive a satisfactory answer, light the candle once again. Say that today's lesson will help fan the flame of the Spirit in their lives.

Absorb the Word (30-35 Minutes)

Defining "Quench"

Use the following questions to cover this section of the discipleship book.

- **How does the *faucet analogy* enhance our understanding of "quenching" the Holy Spirit?**

- How is quenching the Spirit different from grieving Him?

Demonstrating a Quenching of the Holy Spirit

This section of the discipleship book discusses three ways to quench the Spirit: by refusing what He wants to do *for you*, rejecting what He wants to do *in you* and resisting what He yearns to do *through you*.

Refusing His Work *for You*

- According to First Corinthians 2:12, what is one thing the Holy Spirit wants to do for us?

- Who can illustrate how God's Spirit has impressed a particular Bible truth on you or enhanced your understanding of a particular verse?

- Read John 14:16. What does the Spirit's title imply about what He wants to do for us?

- What are some ways in which the Holy Spirit has comforted you in times of special need?

- Look up Romans 8:14. What are some ways in which we need the leading of God's Spirit?

- What are some sources through which the Spirit offers wisdom and guidance?

- Who can share a time when the Holy
  Spirit led or guided him through Bible
  study, prayer or the counsel of other believers?

Rejecting His Work *in You*

- How does the phrase "from the inside out"
  describe the emphasis of this section?

- Why are attitudes and motives a pivotal
  battleground in the warfare between the
  flesh and the spirit?

- How does the maxim "We are responsible
  for our response" relate to "inside jobs"
  that the Holy Spirit wants to perform?

Resisting His Work *through You*

- What is the ultimate purpose of God
  working for us and in us?

- How do the following Bible passages
  summarize what the Spirit wants to do
  through us? a) Matthew 5:13-16; b)
  Matthew 28:18-20; c) Acts 1:8; d) Second Corinthians 5:19-20.

Deterrents to Quenching the Spirit

- How do the fuel and oxygen analogies relate to the working of the Holy Spirit in
  our lives?

- Which sentence from the commentary in
  the discipleship book best summarizes for

you how Scripture and the Holy Spirit work in tandem? (Direct their attention to pages 78-79 in the discipleship book.)

- How does the doctrine of creation validate the "still small voice" of the Holy Spirit?

- How can we tell whether or not inward impressions are from the Holy Spirit?

- Read aloud this sentence from page 79 of the discipleship book: *Don't equate "inner promptings" or "subjective impressions" with new revelation from God.* Why is that statement so integral to a discussion of "inner promptings"?

- Which characteristic of the Holy Spirit's promptings stood out most to you? Why?

Apply the Word (12-15 Minutes)

The organizational framework for the Bible study in this lesson is the following outline. You quench the Holy Spirit by

- Refusing His work *for you*

- Rejecting His work *in you*

- Resisting His work *through you*

At the end of these three subsections in the discipleship book, participants answered application questions that have not yet been covered in your group meeting. At this time, divide into smaller groups of two or three people. Instruct the group to share their written responses to those exercises.

(They described times when they've quenched the Spirit's work for them, in them and through them.) Also give them unhurried time for intercessory prayer as they seek to help each other fan the flames of the Spirit instead of quenching Him.

Before dispersing, point out that one way we reject His work in us is to ignore the conviction of the Spirit in response to sin. Robertson McQuilkin made the following comments regarding the significant ministry of the Spirit *in us*. Read his remarks aloud:

> My friend Pramod had a disease—a form of leprosy. . . . [H]e could feel no pain in his hands and feet. Pramod caused himself serious injuries, eventually hastening his own death, because of his lack of feeling. A person with leprosy may feel no pain, but the absence of pain is harmful rather than good.
>
> Apart from the convicting work of the Spirit, we are something like Pramod—only ours is a form of spiritual leprosy, deadening our sensitivity to sin.[1]

Looking Ahead

To stimulate interest in Chapter 7, read aloud the first paragraph of the chapter, being sure to emphasize that Chapter 7 tells what it means for the Spirit to "have a monopoly" on a person.

LEADERSHIP TIP
Assimilating New Group Members

You may have had a new person join the group after the first few sessions. How well was he assimilated? To assimilate means to absorb into a system or into the cultural tradition of a particular group of people. Assimilation occurs in a group when a new person feels welcome and quickly shifts from marginal commitment to consistent participation in the group. To determine how well your group assimilates a new person, mull over the following questions:

- *What words described the behavior of the "regulars" toward the new person? Why?*

- *What strategies do I employ to create a better sense of belonging and improve assimilation?*

What Does It Mean to Be "Filled with the Holy Spirit"?

Lesson Theme and Objectives

What do you associate with the phrase "the filling of the Holy Spirit"? The phrase connotes different things to different people, depending on their church background or experiences. Some Christians cringe when they see or hear the phrase because they think of controversial manifestations of the Spirit's influence and they try to avoid the subject altogether.

But Scripture won't allow us to neglect the topic. Ephesians 5:18 commands us to "be filled with the Spirit." So it is necessary to determine what God Himself associates with the concept. Lessons 7 and 8 will help to crystallize group members' thinking on this pivotal issue. This lesson focuses on understanding the concept, whereas the next one will discuss how to experience it. Allow the following objectives to serve as a guiding mechanism for coverage of Chapter 7.

1. To define what the Holy Spirit's filling *is* as well as what it *isn't*.

2. To identify biblical evidences of the Holy
   Spirit's filling.
3. To evaluate our spiritual walk in light of biblical evidences of the Spirit's control.

Group Accountability (3-5 Minutes)

Tell participants to pair off and recite Ephesians 5:18 to one another. Discuss: **Ephesians
5:18 is a command. What are the implications of
this grammatical form for our lives?**

Approach the Word (3-5 Minutes)

Discuss: **What are some misconceptions people
have concerning the filling of the Holy Spirit?
How do these misconceptions hinder people's experience of the Spirit's filling?**

To provide transition into the lesson, point out
that this Bible study and the next should erase most
misconceptions and facilitate our day-to-day experience of the Holy Spirit's control.

Absorb the Word (30-35 Minutes)

To Cover "What Is the
Holy Spirit's 'Filling'?"

- **What one word summarizes the concept
  of the Holy Spirit's "filling"?**

- **Imagine that you hear a believer say, "I
  want more of the Holy Spirit." How would
  you respond to him? Why?**

- What one sentence from this section of the discipleship book does the most to clarify this truth for you?

How Does the Holy Spirit's "Filling" Show?

From their study of five Bible passages, participants uncovered seven evidences of the Spirit's filling:

- a heartfelt capacity to worship
- a grateful attitude
- authentic fellowship with other believers
- a new capacity and desire to overcome sinful habits
- a greater desire and power for service
- a greater appetite for and understanding of God's Word
- a zeal for sharing your faith

To encourage creative reflection on the Bible study exercises, divide the group into smaller groups. **Instruct members of each smaller group to select one or two of the seven evidences listed above and create a skit in which the evidence(s) is either demonstrated or lacking in the life of a Christian.** Their task is to come up with a realistic situation from the context of work, school, family relationships or church gatherings. Their hypothetical circumstances and/or dialogue would present an opportunity to exhibit either an evidence of the

Spirit's control or, by contrast, to show a more
"fleshly" response. (It is even conceivable that in the
same dramatic presentation one person will demonstrate one or two evidences of the Spirit's control,
whereas a different participant will respond in a
more carnal manner.)

Give the smaller groups ten to twelve minutes
to plan their presentations but no more than three
to five minutes each to present it. **After each skit,
ask others to identify which of the seven evidences were either illustrated or lacking.**

Alternate activity: Some of your group members may not feel comfortable acting in skits. If
this is the case, use the questions that follow to
examine the seven evidences of the Spirit's filling.

Regarding "a heartfelt capacity to worship"

- **How do the authors of the discipleship
  book define "worship"?** (See page 90 of
  the discipleship book.)

- **What are some attributes of God that you
  are aware of from personal Bible study
  that make Him worthy of worship?**
  (Don't feel you need to limit yourself to
  the content of Chapter 7 in the book.)

- **What divine trait means most to you right
  now? Why?**

Regarding "a grateful attitude"

- **What are some attitudes and actions that
  stand in stark contrast to a grateful spirit?**
  (See page 91 of the discipleship book.)

- What is something specific that you want to give God public thanks for today?

Regarding "authentic fellowship with other believers"

- Why is the Spirit's filling integral to meaningful fellowship? (See page 92 of the discipleship book.)

- What are some expressions of fellowship that require the Spirit's control?

- Who can illustrate how the Spirit has ministered to you through the means of Christian fellowship?

Regarding "a new capacity and desire to overcome sinful habits"

- According to Galatians 5:16-25, why is the Holy Spirit's power so integral to holiness?

- Next, read aloud the following poem. Point out how it reveals a heartfelt reliance on the Holy Spirit for holiness:

Holy Spirit, Light Divine

Holy Spirit, Light divine,
Shine upon this heart of mine;
Chase the shades of night away,
Turn my darkness into day.

Holy Spirit, Power divine,
Cleanse this guilty heart of mine;
Long has sin without control
Held dominion o'er my soul.

Holy Spirit, Joy divine,
Cheer this saddened heart of mine;
Bid my many woes depart,
Heal my wounded, bleeding heart.

Holy Spirit, All divine,
Dwell within this heart of mine;
Cast down every idol throne,
Reign supreme, and reign alone.
                              —Andrew Reed[1]

Regarding "a greater desire
and power for service"

- **According to First Corinthians 12:4-6, why is the Spirit's work integral to effective ministry?**

- **Who can share a time when his direct reliance on the Holy Spirit resulted in fruitful ministry?**

Also read aloud the following testimony of a Christian author regarding the link between the Spirit and powerful service:

> When I write, I'm always grateful to note any small amount of "fruit" God gives. But once in a while the words flow almost uninvited out of my computer like they're on fire. When published, the work seems to take on a life of its own. When I read it later I say, "Where'd that come from? Did I write that?" The Spirit had been working that day, and the result wasn't just my work.[2]

Regarding "a greater appetite for and understanding of God's Word"

- Based on Second Peter 1:19-21, why is an appetite for Scripture a logical outcome of the Spirit's filling? (See page 94.)

- How can we express our dependence on the Spirit for an understanding of Scripture? (Refer to the prayer in Psalm 119:18.)

- Read Acts 16:14, which describes Paul's evangelistic ministry in Philippi. **What phrase from this verse reveals the necessary work of God's Spirit in the process of conversion?** (Point out that the Lord—not Paul—opened Lydia's heart.)

Regarding "a zeal for sharing your faith"

- Read Second Timothy 1:7. God is not the source of crippling fear or timidity that restricts our involvement in personal evangelism. **If a person is shackled by a fear to witness, what does that imply about the filling of the Holy Spirit in his life?**

Apply the Word (12-15 Minutes)

Personal Reflection

In pairs or groups of three, ask participants to share their written responses to the four questions in this segment of the discipleship book. Emphasize that every Christian is "in process." As we grow we yield more and more of our lives to Him. Honest answers to the questions may reveal that members

haven't "arrived," spiritually speaking. That's OK—
so long as they're headed in the right direction! Be
sure participants pray for each other before dispersing.

Looking Ahead

Assign Chapter 8. Read aloud the quote above
the chapter title, the one starting with the words,
"Being filled with the Spirit is not. . . ." (See page 99
of the discipleship book.) Point out that the lesson
on *how* to be filled with the Spirit teems with ideas
for deepening our relationship with the Lord.

LEADERSHIP TIP
Notice the Nonverbal

Whether you're engaged in a casual conversation or leading a discipleship group or Bible study, your communication
comes across through three modes: *actual words, tone of
voice* and *nonverbal cues.* A wise communicator realizes
that his message travels on all three avenues of expression.
To maximize effectiveness he packages his message in a way
that utilizes all three modes.

You may be surprised at how little impact your words
themselves make. Experts on communication theory insist that *how* we say something packs more of a wallop
than *what* we say. Here's how one report breaks it down:

> In a conversation or teaching situation, seven percent of
> our message is conveyed through words, thirty-eight
> percent through tone of voice, and fifty-five percent
> through nonverbal signs.[3]

Just think—both tone of voice and nonverbal signals affect the communication of our message to a much greater extent than our vocabulary. Our *nonverbal* reinforcement is significantly more potent than our verbal feedback.

When is your nonverbal communication most potent? While others in your discipleship group are talking? As they answer or ask questions, what message is your body language sending? Do you come across as tense or relaxed? As interested or impatient? What you say without using your vocal chords can either fan the flames of group participation or throw icy water on them.

How Can I Be Filled with the Holy Spirit?

Lesson Theme and Objectives

The previous lesson emphasized that the filling of the Holy Spirit is a matter of *control*. A Christian cannot get more of the Holy Spirit but the Spirit can get more of him. Group members explored evidences of the Spirit's control, then evaluated their relationship with Him in light of those evidences. Now the spotlight shifts to application: *What perspectives and practices are needed to put a believer under the control of the Holy Spirit?* The following objectives offer direction for this group meeting.

1. To explain how the filling of the Spirit is both a work of God as well as a human responsibility.
2. To identify concrete strategies for facilitating the Spirit's work in our lives.
3. To evaluate our current experience in view of the means God has provided for a Spirit-filled life.

Group Accountability (6-8 Minutes)

Review the seven evidences of the Spirit's filling from Lesson 7: *a heartfelt capacity to worship, a*

grateful attitude, authentic fellowship with other be-
lievers, a new capacity and desire to overcome sinful
habits, a greater desire and power for service, a
greater appetite for and understanding of God's
Word and *a zeal for sharing your faith.* Seek brief
volunteer testimonies in response to the following
question: **Since we last met, who can share how he
has experienced one or more of these evidences?**

Next, pair off and instruct everyone to recite
Luke 11:13 from memory.

Approach the Word (5-7 Minutes)

Put the following statement on a marker board
or chalkboard:

Holiness is entirely a work of God in our lives.

Ask for volunteer responses to these questions:
Do you agree or disagree with the statement? Why?

When this question is posed, it is customary to
receive replies on both sides of the issue. Rather
than give your answer or any definitive reply at
this time, provide transition into the lesson with
remarks similar to the following: *Holiness is impossible without a work of God's Spirit in our
lives. However, as we will see in today's study, we
also have responsibilities in the process of sanctifi-
cation. So no matter how you answer the question,
you have a valid point to make. Like holiness, the
concept of "being filled with the Spirit" is a divine
work. Human effort alone won't fill us with the
Holy Spirit. Yet we will see that we do have re-*

sponsibility. God gives us the freedom to choose whether or not we allow Him to fill us.

Absorb the Word (30-35 Minutes)

God's Part . . . and Yours

- How does Ephesians 5:18 reveal God's initiative in filling us with His Spirit?

- What aspects of Ephesians 5:18 suggest human responsibility in being "filled with the Spirit"?

- How does Galatians 6:8 help us understand the divine and human roles in the process of spiritual development?

- Which one or two sentences from the commentary in this section (pages 100-102) help crystallize "God's part . . . and yours" in living a Spirit-filled life?

Sowing to the Spirit

The six ways to "sow to the Spirit" are covered in six subsections in the discipleship book. The first letter of each strategy forms the acrostic FILLED. Use the following questions to probe those steps in sequence. The material in the discipleship book will provide grist for group members' thinking.

- Instruct participants to read First John 1:9. **Why is an ongoing habit of confessing sin necessary?**

- What does the term "confess" imply about our attitude toward sin? (See definition on page 102 of the discipleship book.)

- Read aloud this maxim: *A throne has a seating capacity of just one.* What strategy does that maxim suggest for facilitating the Spirit's work in our lives?

- Why is a one-time act of surrender insufficient for long-term Spirit-filled living?

- What role does leaning on God's promises play in living a Spirit-filled life?

- Which quotation on the role of faith impresses you most? Why? (See pages 106-108 of the discipleship book.)

- If you're tired of living in spiritual poverty, what simple steps do the authors recommend? (See pages 109-110 of the discipleship book.)

- Look at the second paragraph in the "Express Your Desire for the Spirit's Filling" subsection (page 109). What words would you use to describe the prayer?

- When it comes to Christian living, what is the difference between faith and feelings? (See pages 110-111 of the discipleship book.)

- Why are human feelings an unreliable indicator of the Holy Spirit's filling? (See page 110 of the discipleship book.)

Apply the Word (6-8 Minutes)

Divide into the same pairs used earlier for the Scripture memory recitation. Instruct each group member to go over "The Heart of the Matter" activity found in the discipleship books with his partner (pages 111-112). (They checked what they've already done to expedite their experiences of the Spirit's filling. Then they put a "W" by steps they're willing to implement.) Give them time to pray for each other's follow-through as indicated by the steps they marked with a "W."

Looking Ahead

Tell your group that it is possible to start the day filled with the Spirit, but to grieve or quench the Holy Spirit before the day is over. In Chapter 9, entitled, "How Can I Walk in the Holy Spirit?" they will learn how to *stay* filled throughout the day.

LEADERSHIP TIP
Body Language

Educational researchers have compared the relative effect of verbal and nonverbal reinforcement in response to student comments. On one occasion, college teachers intentionally sent conflicting reinforcement messages as a way of determining which mode students perceived as more powerful.

In one group, the teacher displayed positive nonverbal reinforcement (smiled, maintained eye contact, indicated positive attitude to student answers with facial and body cues) but, at the same time, sent out negative verbal messages. In the second case, the process was reversed, and negative nonverbal reinforcement was coupled with positive verbal reinforcement (frowns, poor eye contact and the like coupled with "good," "nice job," etc.).

In both cases the nonverbal reinforcement was accepted as the primary message by the majority of students. Whether the nonverbal message was positive or negative, most students responded to the nonverbal rather than to the verbal reinforcement. This study provides fascinating support to the notion of "silent language" . . . and it emphasizes the importance of teachers attending to what they do not say as well as to what they do say as they reinforce student participation.[1]

Responding to a group member's question or input is "the art of the immediate." It's hard to prepare for because your response requires a number of complex, on-the-spot decisions. It is as much a relational skill as it is a teaching proficiency. With prayerful effort a small group leader or classroom teacher can transmit appropriate, positive nonverbal messages. Consider the following aspects of your nonverbal delivery system.

Body movement and posture: If you are standing as you teach, encourage participation by stepping close to the students when you pose a question. When someone responds, walk to the side of the room where he is sitting. Closing the gap conveys interest in what is being said. If you are sitting, lean forward or inch closer to the edge of your chair whenever others contribute. They'll feel that you're listening with your heart and not just your ears.

Facial expression and eye contact: When your group members participate in a discussion, does your face convey boredom or enthusiasm? Do you nod to let them know you're following their line of thought? Do you rivet your eyes to the person talking or shift them back and forth between the participants and your notes? You may *hear* everything a group member says without looking at him, but *listening* requires eye contact.

How Can I Walk in the Holy Spirit?

Lesson Theme and Objectives

A Christian's life is riddled with spiritual warfare. Foes of the faith such as the world, the flesh and the devil wage a relentless battle for the hearts of God's people. That is why it is possible to start the day filled with God's Spirit and end it by grieving or quenching Him. Put simply, learning how to *walk* in the Spirit is learning how to *stay filled* as the day progresses. The following objectives serve as the organizational framework for this Bible study.

1. To gain a realistic perspective on the inevitability of a spiritual struggle.
2. To identify evidences of walking in the flesh as opposed to walking in the Spirit.
3. To discuss the type of fuel that's needed to keep our hearts burning for the Lord.
4. To examine guidelines for determining whether inner promptings are from the Holy Spirit.
5. To realize that the Spirit's filling is an ongoing process, not a once-in-a-lifetime experience.

6. To understand that walking in the Spirit is a relationship, not a mechanical routine.

Group Accountability (3-5 Minutes)

Meet in pairs. Remind participants that the question covered in Lesson 8—"How Can I Be Filled
with the Holy Spirit?"—was answered with a
six-step strategy. The term FILLED served as an
acrostic that introduced the six steps. Instruct the
pairs to try and recite the steps without looking at
Chapter 8 of their discipleship book. Then tell them
to recite today's memory verse: Galatians 5:16-18.

Approach the Word (4-6 Minutes)

I (Terry) know of a wise grandfather who often
answers questions his teenaged grandson raises
about Christian living. Once, the young man in-
quired about the persistence required in his at-
tempts to follow Christ. He wondered why he had
to keep on praying, to keep on battling temptation.
He wished he could just shoot one heartfelt prayer
off to God and have it last for at least a few days.

The grandfather didn't soften reality for his be-
loved grandson. He exposed the inevitable need for
consistency in the Christian walk when he said,
"Brad, one sure thing about being a disciple of
Christ is that it is daily."

Read aloud the anecdote in the preceding para-
graphs. Then discuss: How does the grandfather's
comment relate to Chapter 9 in your discipleship
book? (Chapter 9 emphasizes the daily walk in the

Spirit that is integral to successful Christian living. Participants learned that spiritual warfare is inevitable and that the Spirit's filling is an ongoing process, not a once-in-a-lifetime experience.

Point out that this lesson helps equip them for the necessary daily process of walking in the Spirit.

Absorb the Word (30-40 Minutes)

The acronym WALK provides the organizational framework for the heart of this lesson. Group members explored four broad strategies for walking in the Spirit, or staying filled with the Spirit. To explore those strategies as a group, employ the ideas that follow.

Watch Out for the Flesh

- **Why is vigilance in daily Christian living necessary?** (The observation exercise based on Romans 13:14, 1 Peter 1:13-15, and 1 Peter 2:11 provides fodder for their thinking.)

Refer to the Bible study questions on King Saul, based on First Samuel 15. Instead of rehashing their recorded answer to every question, obtain the following feedback:

- **What various manifestations of "walking in the flesh" did you see in First Samuel 15?**

Here is a sample of what they might have found:

1. Never forget what God says about the flesh
   (Amalek) (15:1-3).
   Saul was to utterly destroy Amalek (15:3).
2. Self (the flesh) always wants to receive glory
   (15:10-12).
   Saul then built a monument to himself (15:12).
3. One can be easily deceived about self (15:13-14).
   Saul believed he carried out God's command
   (15:13).
4. Self will blame anyone but the right person
   (15:15).
   Saul blamed it on the people (15:15).
5. Another ploy of the flesh is to justify its actions
   (15:16-21).
   *Saul said he did obey the Lord, but the others
   did not follow through completely* (15:20).
6. Saying "yes" to God and "no" to self is a must
   (15:22).
   *Saul learned that obedience is better than sacri-
   fice* (15:22).
7. Living the self-life will produce undesirable
   consequences (15:23-29).
   Saul lost his kingdom (15:28).
8. Dealing with actions (sins) is one thing, dealing
   with the heart (self) is another (15:30-31).
   *Saul asked forgiveness for his actions, but then
   he immediately asked Samuel to honor him*
   (15:30).

   • **What can we learn about dealing with de-
     sires of the flesh from this story?** (Be ruth-
     less   in   your   attitude   toward   self

[15:32-35]. *Samuel hewed Agag, the king of the Amalekites, to pieces.)*

- How does the concept of "guerilla warfare" explain the battle between the flesh and the Spirit? (See page 118 of the discipleship book.)

Attend to Your Heart's Inner Fire

- What is the connection between this step and the chapter on quenching the Holy Spirit? (See page 119.)

- What truth is conveyed by the story about the Eskimo's dogs? (See pages 119-120.)

- Participants examined the role of Scripture in attending to their hearts' inner fire. They received tips for *reading, studying* and *memorizing* God's Word. Seek a couple of brief testimonies from group members who have applied one or more tips offered in the discipleship book. Ask them to identify specific benefits they have experienced. Hearing testimonials of this sort can whet others' appetite for the Bible. Next, divide into pairs and instruct everyone to share which reading, study and memorization tip appeals to him most and why.

- Refer to the practical suggestions for fueling the heart through *prayer* and *church participation.* (See pages 122-123 of the discipleship book.) Discuss: Why is in-

volvement with other believers integral to a
burning heart? Who can illustrate from experience how church participation has
fanned the flames of his Christian commitment?

- Why is "walking in the Spirit" not an in-
stantaneous, automatic experience after
converting to Christ? (Use the discipleship
book analogy of a one-year-old child on
pages 122-123 to supplement their responses.)

Listen to Inner Promptings

- In what sense do "inner promptings" of the
Holy Spirit rely on subjective impressions?
(See pages 124-125.)

- In what sense are reliable inner promptings
rooted in objective truth? (See page 124.)

- This section of the discipleship book offers
a series of evaluative questions for testing
the reliability of inner promptings. (See
pages 125-126 of the discipleship book.)
Which guideline do you find most helpful?
Why?

Keep on Being Filled

Read aloud Ephesians 5:18 using the literal
translation which says, "*Keep on* being filled."
Ask: What is the significance of this literal render-
ing? Though walking in the Spirit can be broken
down into steps, why can it never be routine?

Before moving to the application phase of the lesson, use the acronym WALK to review the four basic strategies for "staying filled" with the Holy Spirit.

Apply the Word (10-12 Minutes)

In smaller groups, ask everyone to share his written responses to the three incomplete sentences at the end of Chapter 9 in the discipleship books. (See pages 129-130 where they were asked to identify the most convicting insight, the most encouraging truth and the point that has the most bearing on their immediate behavior.) Tell them to pray, encouraging each other to follow through regarding the insight that has the most bearing on their current behavior. Encourage them to tell specifically what they plan to do to apply that insight.

Looking Ahead

Assign Chapter 10. Emphasize that one who "walks in the Spirit" manifests certain character traits. Those traits are covered in Chapter 10 on the "fruit" of the Spirit.

LEADERSHIP TIP
Positive Reinforcement

In a small group, positive reinforcement refers to things leaders say and do to reward learner participation. A potent type of reinforcement is expressing enthusiasm over

group members' discoveries. To maximize verbal reinforcement make your praise as specific as possible. Point
out what it was that a person said that you deemed significant. Notice how the following reinforcements emphasize distinctive aspects of group members' contributions.

- *"Excellent answer, Valerie. I like the way you kept referring to Jesus' words to support your conclusions."*

- *"That's a provocative question, Joseph. Sometimes our zeal for God's Word shows more in the questions we ask than in the answers we give. Anyone want to take a shot at Joseph's question?"*

- *"Way to go, Bryan! You did a good job of putting Paul's remark in context."*

- *"Beth, that's good thinking. Could you repeat your answer so we can think about it a little more?" (Turn to others in the group.) "Notice how Beth unites these two episodes. The connection isn't obvious at first glance."*

- *"It is evident you fellows don't see eye-to-eye on this issue. But I appreciate the way you expressed your viewpoints tactfully and listened to each other."*

- *"I'm impressed by the way you connected this verse to last week's lesson."*

How Can I Exhibit
the Fruit of the Holy Spirit?

Lesson Theme and Objectives

One way to tell whether or not we are walking in the Spirit is to determine the extent to which we are demonstrating a distinctively Christian character. If we're controlled by Him on a day-to-day basis it will show in what is called the "fruit" of the Holy Spirit. This lesson inspects the qualities listed in Galatians 5:22-23: love, joy, peace, patience, kindness, goodness, faithfulness, gentleness and self-control. A successful group time will hinge on achievement of the following objectives:

1. To examine the distinctive meaning of each of the nine traits in Galatians 5:22-23.
2. To help group members determine the extent to which they are manifesting each trait.
3. To pray for one another in light of personal needs revealed by the Bible study.

Group Accountability (4-6 Minutes)

The previous lesson focused on how to "walk" in the Holy Spirit. Ask for a couple of volunteer

responses to this question: **What practical difference has the content of Chapter 9 had on your
life?** (Seek reports of ways the study has affected
their thinking, schedules, habits or relationships.)

Next divide participants into pairs and ask everyone to quote Galatians 5:22-24 from memory.
Since you're dealing with three verses, tell one person to recite verse 22, then the other person can recite verses 23-24.

Approach the Word (5-7 Minutes)

Launch the new lesson with the following quotation:

> The main agenda of God's
> Spirit is transformation.[1]

Discuss: **What do you associate with the word
"transformation"? How does this quote relate to
today's topic?** (Emphasize that when the Holy
Spirit transforms us, it shows through the demonstration of character, as described in the "fruit of
the Spirit" in Galatians 5:22-23.)

Absorb the Word (30-35 Minutes)

Study exercises in Chapter 10 of the book define the nine fruit of the Spirit, incorporate other
Scripture verses that address the traits and encourage group members to evaluate their lives in
light of each fruit. Use the following questions for
highlighting important elements within Chapter
10. Supplement volunteer responses as you deem
necessary. Depending on the amount of time you

have available, you may need to select some questions and omit others.

Love

- What distinguishes *agape* love from other types of love such as romantic love or brotherly affection? (See page 135-136 of the discipleship book.)
- According to John 13:34-35, what is the relationship between world evangelism and *agape* love among Christians?

Joy

- What is the essential difference between "joy" and "happiness"? (See pages 137-138.)
- Based on John 15:1-11, what is a prerequisite for experiencing joy?

Peace

- According to Philippians 4:6-7, how does a person move from a state of anxiety to "the peace of God"? (Refer to pages 138-140.)
- Share a time when you observed a Christian who was peaceful in the midst of challenging circumstances.

Patience

- What are some situations when patience is most needed?

- What attribute(s) of God are an essential focus for a person who demonstrates patience?
- From Lamentations 3:25, what strategy does God recommend for the person experiencing delay?

Kindness

- What effect does kindness have on human relationships?

Goodness

- In what way does "goodness" exceed the virtue of "righteousness"?

Faithfulness

- Why do the authors equate faithfulness with "spiritual stick-to-itiveness"?
- What basis do we have for remaining loyal to God during times of drudgery or testing?

Gentleness

- Chapter 10 of the book cites several usages of the Greek term translated "gentleness." Which usage best clarifies the trait of gentleness to you? Why?
- Tell us about a Christian you've encountered who models the trait of gentleness.

Self-Control

- Chapter 10 mentions five areas in which Christians need self-control in order to distinguish them from the world. (See pages 149-151.) **Pick one of those areas. Tell why you think self-mastery in this realm is so important. Perhaps add how God is dealing with you personally in this area.**

Though the topic of spiritual gifts is reserved for the next chapter, at this time read aloud the following comparison of "fruit" and "gifts." Robertson McQuilkin's comments will reiterate the top-shelf priority that God places on the fruit of the Spirit:

> In the most thorough discussion of spiritual gifts in the Bible, 1 Corinthians 12-14, fruit is said to be more important than gifts. Right in the middle of Paul's discussion of gifts, he says, "Now I'm going to describe something far more important than all these gifts combined." Then he gives the magnificent love chapter, 1 Corinthians 13. Love is a fruit. . . . Some say it is a summation of all the fruit of the Spirit.
>
> God intends for all His children to be like Him—to bear all the fruit of the Spirit. Yet, 1 Corinthians 12-14 demonstrated clearly that the Spirit does not give all the gifts to one person. God wants everyone to be completely like Him in character, but not like Him in His abilities. . . . Fruit is for everyone, always; gifts, some to one, some to another.[2]

Apply the Word (12-15 Minutes)

The exercises in Chapter 10 included questions for self-evaluation by learners. Give them a few minutes to review what they wrote in response to the self-assessment questions. Then encourage responses to the following probes. (If your group is large, divide into smaller groups for this sharing time.)

1. What new or fresh insight about the fruit of the Spirit did you glean from this study?
2. What part of the study was most challenging or convicting? Why?
3. In what way did the Lord encourage you during the study?
4. How should the content of this lesson affect your prayer life?
5. Which of the nine fruits of the Spirit is the Lord impressing upon you at this time? Why?

To close, divide into pairs. Ask everyone to pray for and with his partner in light of that person's response to the question: **In what one or two areas are you most lacking self-control?** (See page 151 of the discipleship book.)

Looking Ahead

Assign Chapter 11. Point out that the next Bible study will combat negative attitudes such as inferiority and envy within the church.

LEADERSHIP TIP
Guidelines for Personal Illustrations

A leadership trait that creates an open, honest discipleship group is *transparency*. When a group leader shares how a Bible truth affects him or asks others to intercede on his behalf, others feel more comfortable communicating on a personal level. Even the apostle Paul modeled transparency before the people he led:

> We do not want you to be unaware, brethren, of our affliction which came to us in Asia, that we were burdened excessively, beyond our strength, so that we despaired even of life. . . . We had the sentence of death within ourselves so that we would not trust in ourselves, but in God who raises the dead . . . He will yet deliver us, you also joining in helping us through your prayers. (2 Corinthians 1:8-11)

However, being transparent does not require you to publicize every secret or divulge everything about your private life. Before choosing to share something personal, mull over these six guidelines:

- Will my personal anecdote accelerate Bible learning by clarifying a truth we're covering?

- Will my personal illustration show the benefits of obeying a particular truth or the painful consequences of neglecting it?

- Will my self-disclosure meet a genuine need in my life for emotional support and prayer?

- Will my self-revelation encourage others to share needs and prayer requests?

- Will my illustration portray family members or friends in a negative manner?

- Have I received permission to tell the story from
  the people who could be embarrassed by it?

How Do I Demonstrate the Gifts of the Holy Spirit?

Lesson Theme and Objectives

A logical outcome of the Holy Spirit's control over a person is *usefulness in ministry*. Inner evidences of walking in the Spirit include the fruit of the Spirit (Chapter 10). External evidence includes involvement in ministry, using the competencies instilled by the Spirit. This is an introductory look at spiritual giftedness. While acknowledging the controversial nature of this topic, this lesson emphasizes basic truths agreed upon by almost all followers of Christ. Set your scope on the following objectives:

1. That learners identify the various gifts mentioned in the New Testament.
2. That learners discover the purposes of spiritual gifts.
3. That learners discuss negative attitudes that the Bible's teaching on gifts should eliminate.
4. That group members determine criteria they can use to discover their gift(s).
5. That participants affirm a spiritual gift they have seen demonstrated by someone they know.

Group Accountability (6-8 minutes)

Divide into pairs and instruct one person to recite First Corinthians 12:4-5 from memory, and the other verses 6-7. Use these questions to discuss the content of the memory verses: **How is each member of the Trinity involved in a believer's ministry? What distinguishes the following terms:** *gifts, ministries* **and** *effects*? (*Gifts* are the God-given capacities for service. *Ministries* are the various contexts or roles in which gifts are exercised, such as teaching, evangelism or administration. *Effects* refer to the ultimate impact of someone's gift on the lives of others.)

Approach the Word (7-10 minutes)

Read aloud this maxim: *God always equips us for what He calls us to do.* Ask: **What are some specific examples of this biblical truth?** (Example: God gives enablement to live a pure life and overcome temptation: First Corinthians 10:13; Second Corinthians 10:3-5.)

After several participants respond to the question, emphasize how the maxim applies to God's mandate for ministry. Use verses such as Second Corinthians 5:17-20, Ephesians 2:10 and 4:11-12 to point out God's plan to use every Christian in some form of ministry. Then explain how He equips us for what He calls us to do by bestowing what Scripture calls "spiritual gifts."

Before proceeding to the next phase of the lesson, ask several participants to share how the truth of the maxim makes them feel. Their responses should include words like "secure," "encouraged" or "confident."

Absorb the Word (35-40 minutes)

To Cover "What Should
I Know about Spiritual Gifts?"

Participants compiled a "master list" of gifts mentioned in four New Testament passages. There's no need to rehash that material, but at this point in the lesson, give the commentary that follows. *The exact number of spiritual gifts in the New Testament is not clearly discernible. Christian leaders can't even agree. Leslie Flynn identified nineteen, as revealed by the title of his book,* 19 Gifts of the Spirit. *John Walvoord, former President of Dallas Theological Seminary, says that there are "at least sixteen." Others contend that the New Testament lists of gifts are* representative, *or exemplary, rather than exhaustive. In other words, Scripture lists* some *of the significant capacities for service, but there could be others not specifically mentioned in the key "gift" passages. Proponents of this "representative" viewpoint include Larry Richards and Joe Aldrich. Also, persons from some theological persuasions insist that not all the gifts exercised in the early church are operative today. They deny the current validity of miraculous gifts such as tongues, prophecy and healing. They insist that these gifts had a unique function in that day because the canon of God's revealed truth in the New Testament had not been completed.*

Don't get bogged down on these points, but if your church or pastoral leadership has a particular viewpoint on the number of gifts and their validity for today, *briefly* state that position and refer learners to printed or audio resources for further study. Also refer to *Appendix B*, the authors' perspective on the controversial gift of tongues.

Next, seek responses to question 3 on page 158 of the discipleship book. To supplement their input, emphasize that the analogy of the human body reveals *interdependence* among persons in the church. God never intended for us to go it alone as a Christian. The fact of spiritual giftedness is one illustration of this mutual dependence. Because no individual has all the gifts, everyone is in some way dependent on the gifts and ministries of others in a church.

Now solicit volunteer responses to questions 4 through 6 in this section of the book. (Broad purposes of gifts include personal and corporate maturity; smooth functioning of a local church in relationships and ministry; and ultimately, the glory of God. Of course, these purposes aren't mutually exclusive.)

Supplement group members' general observations in question 5 with this insight: Gifts are *interpersonal*, not just institutional. We exercise many of the gifts in the context of informal relationships—in the home, at work and through association with friends. Official ministry positions or offices in church programs are noble ventures, but it isn't always necessary to serve in an institutional role in order to exercise a spiritual gift.

Teaching on spiritual gifts should eliminate the following attitudes: *inferiority* (everyone is gifted), *pride* (all service capacities originate with God and are given apart from our worthiness), *self-sufficiency* (everyone needs the service of others in the body) and *envy* (we can trust God's reasons for distributing the gifts as He pleases).

To Cover "What Are My Spiritual Gifts?"

Group members examined guidelines for recognizing areas of giftedness. Each is stated in the form of a question which is adapted from Kenneth Gangel's book *Unwrap Your Spiritual Gifts*. Discuss: **Which guideline do you find most helpful in evaluating your gifts? Why?**

They also took a "Spiritual Gifts Test" (Appendix A). At this time, if you have a large group, divide into smaller groups of three to four people. Tell each participant to share with the others the results of his gifts test. Also instruct everyone to answer these questions orally after they reveal their test results: **To what extent did the test confirm your personal belief and experience concerning areas of usefulness? Were you surprised by any test results? (Explain.) How do the test results match the feedback you've received from other Christians who have observed you?**

Also, if your group members are close-knit and have a history of fellowship together, encourage them to point out areas of giftedness or ministry potential they have observed in one another. They may be able to confirm or clarify for one another results from the gifts test.

Questions about Spiritual Gifts

If time permits, let volunteers ask unanswered questions on the theme of spiritual gifts. Address probes that you consider significant for the group as a whole. Refer them to published resources on spiritual gifts available from your church library or local Christian bookstore. Resources we suggest include:

- *Discover Your Ministry Niche* and *How to Discover Your Spiritual Gifts,* available from Sheveland Resources, 4221 Shineway Drive, Ada, MI 49301. 1-800-737-5267.

- *Spiritual Gifts* by Bobby Clinton. (Christian Publications, Inc.)

- *Body Life* by Ray Stedman. (GL/Regal Books)

Apply the Word (10-12 minutes)

Encourage those who aren't currently utilizing their gifts to think of a relationship setting or a local church volunteer position in which his gift may be needed. By taking initiative to serve the Lord with the gift(s) this study has identified, they will accelerate their own spiritual growth as well as meet the needs of others in the church or world. (If your study group is sponsored by a local church, invite a staff member to visit this session to explain ministry opportunities within the church program as well as community involvement projects that the church endorses. You want group members to leave the session with specific service opportunities percolating in their minds.)

Ask participants who are currently serving in some capacity to describe their ministries to the group and tell what spiritual gift(s) they are exercising in that role. Another member of the group can pray for each person's fruitfulness before moving to the next respondent.

Looking Ahead

Assign Chapter 12. Point out that what we associate with the power of the Holy Spirit may not be what Scripture associates with the concept.

LEADERSHIP TIP
The Value of Transparency

Here is Larry Richards' take on the value of a leader's transparency:

> Self-revelation is a strength, not a weakness, in spiritual leadership. The reasons for this are rooted in theology: First, we are to be examples not of perfection, but of a process. Second, we are to reflect the gospel. And the gospel is not "accept Christ and become perfect." The gospel is Jesus saying, "Without me you can do nothing!" (John 15:5). If we misrepresent ourselves as so "strong" that we do not need Jesus, we misrepresent the gospel of God's grace.
>
> None of this detracts in any way from the leader's responsibility to be a good example in godliness. But it

does cut us off from being hypocritical. It eliminates the need to pretend whenever we hurt. In sharing ourselves, in being real with others, they may well see our weaknesses . . . but they will also see Jesus' strength! And it will be encouraging that the transformation Jesus has been working in us can be worked in them as well.[1]

Author Ray Stedman echoes Richards' point:

Our earthliness must be as apparent to others as the power is, so they may see that the secret is not us, but God. That is why we must be transparent people, not hiding our weaknesses and failures, but honestly admitting them when they occur.[2]

Also strive to promote transparency among your group members. Perhaps the wisest approach is to ask for personal reactions to the Bible lesson you're covering. In any given lesson, we employ just one or two such questions. And we reserve questions of this sort for the final minutes of a lesson. People first need Bible content to provide the fuel for their thinking. Here's a list of questions that have been successful for us:

- What personal application or carry-over idea has the Lord given you from this study?

- What personal reasons for praising God does this Scripture passage offer?

- What personal need or issue has the Holy Spirit exposed during this study? How can we pray with you about it?

- Who can illustrate—from personal experience— one of our lesson truths?

- What aspect of this study encourages you the most? Why?

- What part of this study convicts you? Why?

- What fresh, I-never-thought-of-that-before insight did you glean from today's Scripture?

- As we identified timeless truths in today's lesson, perhaps a positive role model came to mind. If so, tell us about this person. How did he apply or demonstrate some point we covered?

- What unresolved questions on this subject matter still goad you?

How Do I Demonstrate the Power of the Holy Spirit?

Lesson Theme and Objectives

In his comprehensive volume on the Holy Spirit, Charles Swindoll states,

> God's Word does not toss around the word for *power* loosely; nor are we personally promised supernatural manifestations on a day-to-day basis . . . if miracles occurred every day they wouldn't be called *miracles* . . . they'd be called *regulars.*[1]

Further, Swindoll links the Holy Spirit's power not to unusual phenomena, but to the apostles' public, unashamed witness to a risen Lord.[2]

That's the point of this lesson. The primary way in which spiritual power is employed in the New Testament is in reference to the spreading of the gospel (Acts 1:8; 1 Corinthians 2:4-5; Colossians 1:28-29; 1 Thessalonians 1:5). This course concludes by declaring that a Spirit-filled Christian aspires to be a "world" Christian, involved in some fashion in impacting culture with the message of salvation. Ask the Lord to accomplish the following objectives.

1. That learners realize that they are called to be Christ's witnesses.
2. That group members identify the basic content elements in what is called the "plan of salvation."
3. That participants identify non-Christians in their spheres of influence.
4. That prayer becomes an integral part of participants' outreach efforts.
5. That participants practice a "One-Verse Method" for sharing the Bible's plan of salvation.

Group Accountability (6-8 minutes)

Divide into pairs and instruct participants to recite Acts 1:8 for their partner. Discuss: **Which came first: a reference to the Spirit's enablement or the mandate to witness? Why is the sequence of those two elements significant?**

Approach the Word (4-6 minutes)

Share the following anecdote. In the nineteenth century, a dynamic evangelist came on the scene in the United States. As a result of his preaching, thousands of people put their faith in Jesus Christ. His crusades spread to numerous other countries. He launched a Bible institute to train vocational Christian workers. Several biographers have chronicled his life and influential ministry. Yet when it came to public usefulness, this man defied the odds. He was obese—not a handsome adornment to a speakers' platform. Because he never finished elementary school, he was a poor speller and clumsy with grammar. A secular reporter in England criticized him for "butchering the King's English." There was no *natural* explanation for his success as an evangelist.

The only explanation for the ministry of Dwight L. Moody was *supernatural*. He demonstrated the truth of this lesson: the power of the Holy Spirit enables ordinary people to participate in the task of world evangelization. Not long after his conversion, Moody and a friend were talking. His acquaintance said, "The world has yet to see what God will do with a man fully dedicated to Him." Moody pondered the comment, then replied: "By the Holy Spirit in me, I'll be that man!"[3]

Moody demonstrated that power for ministry stems from the Holy Spirit, not from our own natural resources. That's the point of this final lesson.

Absorb the Word (20-30 minutes)

Who Does Christ Want to Use?

- What does the word "witness" mean? (See page 167 of the discipleship book.)

- In what sense is every Christian qualified to serve as a witness?

- Why is witnessing often less frequent the longer a person is a believer? (See page 168.)

- When a Christian finds it difficult to name at least six non-Christians whom he knows well, what need does that reveal? (See page 169.)

What Is the Scope of the Church's Responsibility?

- In this section of the discipleship book, we provide statistics on the world's population and the proportion of professing Christians to that population. (See pages 169-170.) What are some reactions you had to these statistics? Why?

- In what sense are the numbers a reason for encouragement?

- In what sense are the figures a catalyst for more prayer and engagement with the world?

- The primary strategy for improving those statistics is the personal witness of Christians to individuals in their spheres of influence. In what additional ways does being a "world Christian" show?

What Resource Enables Us as Witnesses?

- How does Acts 16:11-14 reveal the need for human initiative in evangelism?

- How do these verses reveal the need for the Holy Spirit's power in evangelism?

- If only God the Holy Spirit can open an unbeliever's heart, what is a logical application for us as witnesses? (Emphasize that we exercise our dependence on the Lord's role through prayer. We pray for our own ability to communicate the gospel clearly and accurately. We ask the Lord to prepare the heart of the person who will hear our testimony.)

- Not everyone who witnesses for Christ demonstrates a humble dependence on the Holy Spirit. **How does self-sufficiency express itself in the life of a Christian worker?**

Apply the Word (18-20 minutes)

In the "Marching off the Map" section of the discipleship book, participants were encouraged to pray for and cultivate closer relationships with the non-Christians they named, with the ultimate goal of sharing Christ with them. They were also instructed to study the "One-Verse Method" of personal evangelism based on John 3:16 which is shown in Appendix C of the discipleship book.

Ask: **What is the advantage of an evangelistic method that uses just one verse? How do the graphs (visual aids) enhance the presentation of the gospel?**

Close by dividing into pairs and practice sharing the gospel using John 3:16. After they finish practicing, ask everyone to share with his partner the name of *one* non-Christian for whom he has a burden, and to explain the nature of his association with that person. Instruct everyone to answer this question during the interchange with their partner: **What is the most opportune time and place to utilize the "One-Verse Method" with this person?** Give them several minutes to pray for each other's action plans.

LEADERSHIP TIP
Increasing Intercession

Look over the following ways to enhance the ministry of intercession with your group.

- Tag the following questions on to the end of your Bible studies: *What personal needs has the Holy Spirit exposed during this study? How can we pray with you about those needs?*

- Link times of intercession to lesson application. *In a study Terry led on "The Ministry of Encouragement," everyone shared with a partner the names of people who were experiencing discouraging circumstances. After listing concrete, realistic ways to encourage those in need, everyone prayed for his partner to follow through on at least one idea. If you have a close-knit group, ask everyone to huddle with one or two others before dispersing. They can brainstorm for application ideas and pray for each other's follow-through.*

- Lead a Bible study on the theme of intercessory prayer. *Examine the biblical basis for this expression of group life and discuss ways to exercise in-*

tercession in relation to one another. For instance, Terry's title for Nehemiah 1 is "The Ministry of Intercession." The following questions directed learners into the passage and encouraged application:

- What need prompted Nehemiah's intercession?

- Look at the record of Nehemiah's behavior and words in chapter 1. What character qualities did he possess? Why are these particular traits prerequisites for the ministry of intercession?

- What principles of intercession can we glean from Nehemiah's prayer in 1:5-11?

- What insights from Nehemiah chapter 1 are most applicable to our relationships within this group?

- How can we keep the promise "I'll pray for you" from becoming just another church cliché?

ENDNOTES

COURSE INTRODUCTION

1. Chuck Miller, used in a Spring 1973 chapel message delivered to Wheaton Graduate School.

LESSON 1

1. James I. Packer, *Knowing God* (Downers Grove, IL: InterVarsity Press, 1973), p. 59.

LESSON 2

1. A.W. Tozer, *Born after Midnight* (Camp Hill, PA: Christian Publications, 1989), pp. 61-63.

2. Adapted from Robertson McQuilkin's *Life in the Spirit* (Nashville, TN: Lifeway Press, 1997), pp. 66-67.

LESSON 3

1. J. Sidlow Baxter, as quoted in *Illustrations for Biblical Preaching*, Michael Green, ed. (Grand Rapids, MI: Baker Book House, 1989), p. 190.

2. Roy Zuck, *The Holy Spirit in Your Teaching* (Wheaton, IL: Victor Books, 1984), pp. 44-45.

3. McQuilkin, p. 150.

LESSON 4

1. A.C. Dixon, as quoted in Terry Powell's *Welcome to the Church* (Littleton, CO: Lay Action Ministry Program, 1987), p. 40.

2. J. Oswald Sanders, *The Holy Spirit and His Gifts*, revised and enlarged edition (Grand Rapids, MI: Zondervan, 1970), p. 11.

LESSON 6

1. McQuilkin, p. 69.

L E S S O N 7

1. Andrew Reed, as quoted in McQuilkin, p. 17.
2. McQuilkin, p. 144.
3. This material given in a sermon by Rev. Bill Solomon to the congregation of Cornerstone Presbyterian Church of Irmo, South Carolina in 1986.

L E S S O N 8

1. Myra and David Sadker, "Questioning Skills," in *Classroom Teaching Skills* (Lexington, KY: D.C. Heath Co., 1986), pp. 172-173.

L E S S O N 1 0

1. Charles Swindoll, *Flying Closer to the Flame: A Passion for the Holy Spirit* (Dallas, TX: Word Publishing, 1993), p. 37.
2. McQuilkin, pp. 170-171.

L E S S O N 1 1

1. Larry Richards, *A Theology of Christian Education* (Grand Rapids, MI: Zondervan, 1975), p. 142.
2. Ray Stedman, *Authentic Christianity* (Portland, OR: Multnomah Press, 1973), n.p.

L E S S O N 1 2

1. Swindoll, p. 238.
2. Ibid., p. 237.
3. Adapted from an illustration given by Ronald Dunn in a message to Campus Crusade for Christ staff in 1976.

Bill Jones is president of Crossover Communications International. Crossover is a missions organization helping to fulfill the Great Commission in Eurasia, currently focusing on the countries in the area of the Black Sea. Bill also serves as the program director for the Master of Arts in Missions and the Master of Arts in Leadership at Columbia International University in Columbia, South Carolina. A passionate communicator, Bill has trained thousands of people all around the world to effectively share their faith in Christ.

Terry Powell has a Ph.D. in Education Ministry from Trinity Evangelical Divinity School and teaches Christian Education and Bible at Columbia International University.

CROSSOVER
COMMUNICATIONS
INTERNATIONAL

P.O. Box 211755   Columbia, SC 29221
Phone: (803) 691-0688   Fax: (803) 691-9355
www.crossoverusa.org

Write to Terry Powell or Bill Jones at:
CIU
P.O. Box 3122
Columbia, SC 29230
or call (803) 754-4100